Pros and Cons
TRANSPORTATION
The Impact of Science and Technology

Joseph Harris

Gareth Stevens
Publishing

Please visit our web site at: www.garethstevens.com.
For a free color catalog describing Gareth Stevens Publishing's list of high-quality books, call 1-800-542-2595 (USA) or 1-800-387-3178 (Canada). Gareth Stevens Publishing's fax: 1-877-545-2596

Library of Congress Cataloging-in-Publication Data:

Harris, Joseph, 1982-
    Transportation : the impact of science and technology / Joseph Harris.
        p. cm. — (Pros and cons)
    Includes bibliographical references and index.
    ISBN-10: 1-4339-1990-7   ISBN-13: 978-1-4339-1990-9 (lib. bdg.)
    1. Transportation—Environmental aspects—Juvenile literature. 2. Transportation—History—Juvenile literature. I. Title.
HE147.65.H37 2010
388—dc22   2009012437

This North American edition published in 2010 by Gareth Stevens Publishing under license from Arcturus Publishing Limited.
Gareth Stevens Publishing
A Weekly Reader® Company
1 Reader's Digest Road
Pleasantville, NY 10570-7000 USA

Copyright © 2009 Arcturus Publishing Limited
Produced by Arcturus Publishing Limited
26/27 Bickels Yard
151–153 Bermondsey Street
London SE1 3HA

Gareth Stevens Executive Managing Editor: Lisa M. Herrington
Gareth Stevens Editor: Jayne Keedle
Gareth Stevens Senior Designer: Keith Plechaty

Series Concept: Alex Woolf
Editor and Picture Researcher: Nicola Barber
Cover Design: Phipps Design
Consultant: Miles Hudson

Picture Credits: Corbis: 5 (Werner Forman), 6 (Gianni Dagli Orti), 8 (Gao Xueyu/Xinhua Press), 11 (William Manning), 13 (Charles O'Rear), 14 (Ralph White), 16 (Salvador de Sas/epa), 18 (Walter Bibikow), 22 (Hulton-Deutsch Collection), 23 (Paul Hardy), 25 (Bertrand Rieger/Hemis), 27 (G. Bowater), 29 (Atlantide Phototravel), 31 (John Harper), 33 (Gideon Mendel), 37 (Najlah Feanny), 45 (Underwood & Underwood), 47 (Antoine Gyori/AGP), 49 (Reuters), 50 (Thomas Frey/dpa); Science Photo Library: 39 (David Nunuk), 40 (TRL, Ltd.), 56 (Henning Dalhoff/Bonnier Publications), 58 (David A. Hardy, *Futures: 50 Years in Space*); Shutterstock: Cover (egd), 4 (CROM), 15 (Pieter Janssen), 20 (Richard Goldberg), 28 (Holger Mette), 35 (Konstantin Sutyagin), 41 (Soundsnaps), 42 (robdigphoto).

Cover: Automobiles crowd a busy highway in Los Angeles, California, a city that has ongoing problems with air pollution, smog, and heavily congested roadways.

Every attempt has been made to clear copyright. Should there be any inadvertent omission, please apply to the publisher for rectification.

All rights reserved.

Printed in the United States

1 2 3 4 5 6 7 8 9 15 14 13 12 11 10 09

CONTENTS

CHAPTER 1
The Progress of Transportation 4

CHAPTER 2
Water Transportation 10

CHAPTER 3
Rail Travel 22

CHAPTER 4
Road Transportation 32

CHAPTER 5
Air Travel 44

CHAPTER 6
Future Transportation 52

Glossary 60
Further Information 63
Index 64

CHAPTER 1

The Progress of Transportation

It is hard to imagine life without any form of transportation. Yet for most of human history, people have relied on their feet to take them where they needed to go, and on the strength of their muscles to move objects from one place to another.

Natural Energy

For thousands of years, every form of transportation relied on the use of natural energy, whether provided by humans, animals, or the wind. The domestication of the horse and the invention of the wheel opened up many new possibilities. Horses could be ridden fast over long distances. They were also widely used in battles to pull wheeled war chariots. The first vessels on water were primitive rafts but, over time, shipbuilding technology developed. Around 3200 B.C., the Egyptians began to equip their ships with sails.

Over the centuries, people continued to innovate. Stirrups, bridles, and iron horseshoes made riding horses more efficient. Rudders and compasses on ships improved steering and navigation. Horse-drawn vehicles, from wagons to carriages and coaches, gradually became faster and more comfortable. The construction of roads, bridges, and canals

Wheels with spokes were first used around 2000 B.C.

Wheeling Forward

The invention of the wheel was one of the greatest advancements in human history. The earliest images of wheeled vehicles, dated around 3500 B.C., come from the ancient civilization of Sumer (present-day Iraq). Those images show solid wooden wheels on war chariots and on other vehicles that are possibly wagons. Around 2000 B.C., lighter, more maneuverable wheels with spokes began to appear in the Middle East. Wheeled vehicles have played a huge role in trade and war. Yet the inhabitants of the Americas and Australia did not use wheeled vehicles until they were introduced by Europeans in the 16th century.

created better transportation links. Beginning in the 15th century, Europeans learned to build ships that could sail far from land across the oceans. European sailors ventured to America and traveled around Africa to reach the East by sea.

This artifact, the Royal Standard of Ur, dates from about 2500 B.C. Mosaics on this panel depict warriors and chariots. The chariot wheels are filled in — spokes were a later invention.

New Kinds of Power

In the 18th century, wealth, trade, and technological progress combined to produce one of the greatest periods of change in human history. Britain became the first country to fully experience the Industrial Revolution. During that time, machines took over much of the work that had previously been done by humans and animals. One of the key inventions of the Industrial Revolution was the first efficient steam engine, designed by James Watt in 1769. Since the late 18th century, many forms of motive, or moving, power based on steam, oil, and electricity have revolutionized transportation and transformed human progress.

TRANSPORTATION

This print shows the *Rocket*, George Stephenson's pioneering steam locomotive.

Steam Power

According to legend, James Watt saw steam pouring from the spout of a boiling kettle and realized that he might be able to use the force of steam to drive machines. Watt's steam engines were based on that principle. Coal was burned in a furnace to heat quantities of water. The resulting steam was forced through valves, devices that can open or shut to control the flow of steam. The pressure of the steam pushed pistons, metal rods that move up and down. The up and down movement of the pistons worked the engine. The first steam engines were used to drive machinery in mills and factories. However, experiments showed that steam could also move vehicles. Within a few years, steam engines were being used to power both trains and ships.

The Age of Oil

On the roads of Europe and America, horse-drawn vehicles crowded the streets until the late 19th century. That situation began to change in the 1880s, with the development of the internal combustion engine. Internal combustion means "inside burning." That engine ran on a mixture of fuel and air that burned continuously inside a metal tube. This continuous combustion released the energy to push pistons and power the engine. The internal combustion engine was far more compact than a steam engine and enabled the development of the motor car.

Car manufacturers soon found that fuels made from oil, such as gasoline and diesel, were most suitable for the internal combustion engine. Those fuels were soon used to power not only cars, but also ships, trains, and planes. In this way, oil became the world's most important fuel. It remains crucial to the entire global economy, although there are increasing concerns about the effect its use has on the world's environment and climate.

VIEWPOINT

What All the World Desires

The Scottish inventor and engineer James Watt went into partnership with businessman Matthew Boulton and opened a factory to manufacture steam engines. Boulton had no doubts about the value of the new technology. In 1776, he told a visitor to the factory:

"I sell here, sir, what all the world desires to have — power!"

Power at a Price

Coal, oil, and natural gas are all fossil fuels. Fossils are the remains of plants and creatures that existed hundreds of millions of years ago. Layers of coal and oil represent huge numbers of plants and tiny creatures that have been crushed by enormous geological pressure onto rocks and liquids. Because of their origin as living things, oil and coal consist mainly of carbon. Carbon is a building block of life — and a vital fuel source for present-day societies. Since fossil fuels were created over many millions of years, they are a non-renewable fuel. That means they cannot be replaced. There are fears that within a few decades there will be no coal, oil, or natural gas remaining.

TRANSPORTATION

Another problem with the use of fossil fuels is that burning them produces pollutant gases. Those emissions harm both people and the environment. The constant burning of coal blackened many 19th-century cities and is still a significant pollutant in some countries. However, most experts regard oil as the greatest modern pollutant. Emissions from traffic and industry cause chronic air pollution in many cities around the world. For example, air pollution was an issue in 2008 when the Olympic Games were held in Beijing, the capital of China. The Chinese authorities were so concerned about the air quality in Beijing that they decreased car traffic by 50 percent until the end of the games. Owners of cars with odd-numbered registrations were allowed to drive only on odd-numbered dates, while drivers with even-numbered registrations were similarly restricted to driving only on even-numbered dates.

The use of fossil fuels is also blamed for climate change. Global temperatures are rising. Most scientists believe that is happening because such huge quantities of fossil fuels are being burned. The fuels emit

Traffic clogs roadways in Beijing, the capital of China. Pollution from traffic is a major problem for the city.

"greenhouse gases," particularly carbon dioxide (CO_2), which trap heat from the Sun in Earth's atmosphere. The predicted consequences of global warming include melting polar ice caps, rising sea levels, and increasingly extreme weather conditions.

Electric Power

Electricity has important advantages as a form of power. Any form of transportation powered by electricity is less polluting and quieter than types powered by gasoline or diesel. However, other forms of energy are needed to produce electricity. Both coal and oil are burned to generate electricity at power stations, which supply homes, businesses, and some types of transportation. Although electricity is clean at the point of use, its production still involves the burning of polluting fuels.

Going Electric

Electricity is generated at power stations, so it has to be linked to any type of transportation it drives. One method is to transmit electricity through "live" rails, or overhead wires. Many city transportation networks, such as subway systems and tramlines, are powered in this way. A large vehicle, such as a train, can carry the fuel it needs and use it in combination with its own independent generator to produce electricity. Smaller vehicles, such as electric cars, operate by using batteries, which have to be recharged regularly.

 PROS: TRANSPORTATION TECHNOLOGY

Each new development in transportation has enabled people to travel faster and farther. People have explored the world and settled in new regions. Technological advancements have made global trade and travel possible and have increased human productivity and prosperity.

 CONS: TRANSPORTATION TECHNOLOGY

Since the late 19th century, transportation has largely depended on fossil fuels, such as coal and oil. Supplies of both are limited. Burning fossil fuels has polluted the environment and may be causing climate change. Many people believe that the age of oil must end and technology must change to keep humans on the move.

9

CHAPTER 2

Water Transportation

Throughout history, water has played a vital role in the transportation of passengers and cargo. Before the arrival of motorized transportation, the most efficient way to carry heavy goods, such as coal from a mine, was along rivers. In some places where there was no river nearby, people dug an artificial waterway called a canal, to link the place where the goods were produced to the nearest river or port.

Artificial Waterways

People have dug canals since ancient times. Construction of the world's longest artificial waterway, the Grand Canal in China, was started as early as the 300s B.C. That canal was built to transport grain from the farmlands in the south of China to the cities of the north. In Britain, the heyday of canal building coincided with the Industrial Revolution. A national network of canals was rapidly built to transport coal and goods. In the United States, major projects such as the Erie Canal, which opened in 1825 to connect New York City and Buffalo, became thriving trade routes. Canals became less important for transporting goods as railways and roads developed into faster and more efficient alternatives for moving freight. However, many artificial waterways remain in use today.

Lock Gates

Locks are ingenious yet simple devices that enable canals to be built across ground that is not flat. A lock is a short section of a canal with gates at either end. When a boat passes into the lock, the lock gates are shut behind it. Small panels in the lock, called sluice gates, allow water either to pour in or out, depending on whether the boat needs to go up or down. As the water level changes, the boat rises or falls with it. When the water level in the lock is the same as that on the far side of the lock gates, the gates are opened and the boat passes through. In places with steep inclines, a series of locks joined together allows a boat to move smoothly uphill or downhill.

Water Transportation

The locks of the Rideau Canal, in Canada, were built in the 19th century and have been in operation ever since. The canal connects the Canadian cities of Ontario and Kingston.

Oceangoing vessels use ship canals that link inland ports to the sea, or connect two seas or oceans. Some ship canals dramatically reduce the time it takes to complete a voyage. For example, the Suez Canal in Egypt, which opened in 1869, connects the Red Sea to the Mediterranean. Before its construction, ships sailing between the Far East and Europe had to sail around the southern tip of Africa. Similarly, the Panama Canal in Central America, which opened in 1914, links the Atlantic and Pacific Oceans. That 50-mile (80-kilometer) waterway shortens voyages by thousands of miles for ships sailing between the east and west coasts of America.

PROS: CANALS

The construction of canals during the Industrial Revolution had a positive economic impact, decreasing the cost of transporting heavy goods. Canals also helped shape local economies. The Erie Canal encouraged settlement of the Great Lakes region. The canal also promoted the growth of New York City by providing an outlet for the fast shipment of imported goods that came into the United States through its harbor.

 CONS: CANALS

Building canals was difficult and dangerous work. Before the introduction of modern engineering techniques and safety precautions, landslides were a constant danger for workers constructing a canal. Canals also dramatically changed the landscape, redirecting natural water sources, and negatively affecting habitats and the environment.

The Origins of Modern Shipping

The history of modern shipping begins with the development of steam-powered ships in the late 18th century. Earlier ships had relied on oars and wind power. Steamships were propelled by mechanical engines. As a result, they were faster and better able to make their way against winds and currents.

Most early steamships were paddle boats, in which the engine drove a large circular set of paddles either at the back or on the sides of the ship. Those paddle steamers were vulnerable in rough seas because their engines and their large paddle wheels were easily damaged. At first, such ships were fitted with sails in case something went wrong with the engine. Nevertheless, in 1838, one of those paddle steamers, the SS *Sirius*, became the first vessel that used only steam power to cross the Atlantic Ocean from London to New York.

In 1843, the first propeller-driven iron ship, the SS *Great Britain*, was launched. A ship's propeller is a spiral of rotating blades that is fully

Water Transportation

The paddle steamer *Delta Queen* leaves Natchez, Mississippi. From the 19th century, paddle boats linked communities along the Mississippi River.

submerged in the water at the bottom of the hull. The propeller proved far superior to the paddle wheel for powering oceangoing craft because it was not lifted out of the water by the waves. Paddle steamers remained in service for some years on inland waterways, however, most famously transporting passengers and cargo up and down the Mississippi River in the United States.

By the late 19th century, steamships were replacing sailing ships as carriers of cargo throughout the world. Improvements to steam engines continued to increase speed and fuel efficiency. From about 1920, the steam was produced by burning the fuel that would dominate future transportation — oil.

Submarines

In the 17th century, a Dutchman named Cornelius van Drebel built the first submarine. It was propelled by oars and traveled very close to the surface of the water. A tube poked up into the air so that the people inside could breathe! However, the first effective submarines date from the late 19th century. In order for a submarine to dive below the surface of the ocean, large tanks in the ship's hold, called ballast tanks, are filled with water to increase its weight. When it is time to surface again, compressed air is blown into the ballast tanks to force the water out and decrease the vessel's weight.

TRANSPORTATION

 PROS: STEAMSHIPS

Steamships played a vital role in the expansion of world trade during the 19th century. Fleets of merchant ships carried raw materials and mass-produced goods across the globe, while other steamers carried immigrants from Europe across the Atlantic Ocean to settle in the United States.

 CONS: STEAMSHIPS

People who worked on steamships were poorly paid and their jobs were often dangerous. Many lives were lost at sea. Many accidents happened because vessels were overloaded. In 1875, a British member of parliament, Samuel Plimsoll, championed legislation to restrict how much weight could be loaded into a ship. As a result, the Merchant Shipping Act of 1876 introduced legal restrictions on the volume of cargo that could be carried. The line on a ship that indicated when the limit had been reached became known as the Plimsoll line.

Taken in 1986, this underwater photograph shows the hull of the shipwrecked *Titanic* lying on the seabed, 11,975 feet (3,650 meters) below the surface.

Titanic Disaster

The *Titanic* was a steamship that was supposed to combine luxury with an engineering design that made it unsinkable. But on its first voyage, in 1912, the *Titanic* hit an iceberg and sank in the Atlantic Ocean. The impact of the iceberg caused a large area of the hull to buckle and water to pour in. The ship's hull was divided into compartments, each of which was supposed to be watertight. However, the barriers between the sections were not high enough. The water destabilized the ship and, as it leaned over, water flooded from section to section. The *Titanic* sank rapidly. Of the 2,222 passengers and crew on board, only 705 people survived.

Water Transportation

Shipping Cargo

Present-day cargo ships face competition from other methods of carrying freight. Yet they continue to take raw materials and finished products to destinations around the world. No rival form of transportation can match the volume of cargo they can carry or the price at which they can carry it. Many kinds of cargo are carried in special containers, designed to protect the goods inside. The development in the 20th century of standard sizes for shipping containers was of particular importance, as it enabled ships to be filled to capacity.

Currently, the largest container ships are those of the Emma Maersk class, measuring 13,500 twenty-foot equivalency units (TEU). That means those ships can carry up to 13,500 standard containers that measure 20 feet (6.1 meters) by 8 feet (2.4 meters) by 8.5 feet (2.6 meters). Some coastal cities have become centers for the handling and transfer of containers. Examples include Singapore and Shanghai, China, which are two of the busiest ports in the world.

Modern container ships can carry incredible amounts of cargo.

TRANSPORTATION

Bulk Cargo

Not all cargo is carried in containers. The other main type of cargo, called bulk cargo, is carried loose. Many raw materials including grain, coal, and oil are shipped in this way. Oil is transported all around the world in special ships called tankers. Modern oil tankers are enormous, carrying hundreds of thousands of tons of oil. Some people object to those

Oil Spills

In 2002, the tanker *Prestige* spilled its oil off the coast of Spain, causing extensive environmental damage. Environmentalists again called for an immediate ban on single-hulled oil tankers:

"To permit the use of just one thin single sheet of steel [a single hull] to keep huge volumes of toxic petroleum away from the valuable living marine resources on which our coastal economies depend is an obsolete [out-of-date] transportation strategy. Recent events make it crystal clear that the time has come to accelerate the transition to double-hulled tankers."

(Richard Charter, Marine Conservationist)

VIEWPOINT

A worker cleans oil spilt by the tanker *Prestige* in 2002. Only through the painstaking efforts of workers can spills such as this be contained and environmental damage limited.

supertankers because they can damage the environment if there is an accident at sea. During the 20th century, there were more than 200 recorded incidents involving oil tankers. A well-known example is the *Exxon Valdez*, which in 1989 spilled more than 10.5 million gallons (40 million liters) of oil off the coast of Alaska, causing enormous damage to the wildlife and coastline.

Disasters such as the *Exxon Valdez* accident led to new international agreements to replace single-hulled oil tankers with double-hulled designs. A double-hulled ship has an outer and an inner hull, so any impact would have to break through both hulls before the ship spilled its oil. From 2010, all oil tankers are supposed to be double-hulled. However, because it is so expensive to replace those enormous ships, many of those in service remain outdated. Some countries have expressed their intention to allow the continued use of single-hulled oil tankers past the cutoff date.

PROS: CONTAINER SHIPS AND SUPERTANKERS

Today's methods of carrying cargo are extremely efficient. It is much cheaper to move a single large quantity of freight than to fuel and crew many smaller vessels. Those savings are passed on to consumers and help keep prices low. In the specific case of oil, that efficiency is especially important in view of ever-increasing demand. Shipping can become a central aspect of local economies. For example, Shanghai's busy port has helped it to become the commercial center of China.

CONS: CONTAINER SHIPS AND SUPERTANKERS

The huge volume of containers passing through modern ports makes thorough inspection difficult. Most containers are not, in fact, opened. That makes it hard to prevent smuggling of illegal goods, such as drugs or weapons, for use by terrorists. Sometimes, even people are smuggled in containers, though they risk death by suffocation while they are inside.

TRANSPORTATION

Ferries

Ferries are vessels that regularly transport passengers, and sometimes their vehicles, across bodies of water. In many parts of the world ferries provide vital links to islands and, in some places, they form part of a city's public transportation system. For example, many waterways divide the city of Stockholm, the capital of Sweden, so ferries are a natural means of getting around. Ferries also serve different areas of New York City, and are much-used links between the United Kingdom and Europe.

Many modern ferries are either hovercraft or hydrofoils. Both designs have their hulls lifted out of the water to reduce resistance to their passage. The hovercraft, which came into service in the 1960s, uses

Passengers and vehicles ride a ferry to Martha's Vineyard in Massachusetts. Ferries are a vital part of local transportation systems in many parts of the world.

powerful fan engines to lift the vessel and create a cushion of air beneath it. The air is contained by a semicircular barrier, called the skirt. Hydrofoils have a wing-shaped structure, called a foil, which lies under the main hull and lifts it above the surface of the water. Only the foil touches the water, its streamlined shape reducing resistance to a minimum.

Ships are used as ferries, in particular for carrying vehicles across bodies of water. Those ferries are designed so that passengers can drive straight on to the ship through one end and off through the other end. Those roll-on roll-off ferries are often called ro-ros for short.

Catamarans

The original design of a catamaran — two canoes linked together by wooden poles — comes from the Pacific islands of Polynesia. It is remarkably stable even in rough Pacific waters. Western boatbuilders adapted the Polynesian design by turning the canoes into twin hulls. In the 1970s, the catamaran shape was adapted to build ferries. With the hulls reduced to thin blades cutting through the water and the passenger area carried high above them, catamarans became increasingly streamlined vessels.

PROS: ROLL-ON ROLL-OFF FERRIES

Ferries provide a convenient way for people to cross small bodies of water. They eliminate the need for plane travel over short distances. Ro-ros also enable people to take their vehicles from one place to another.

CONS: ROLL-ON ROLL-OFF FERRIES

The ro-ro design has drawbacks. Ro-ro ferries have large entry and exit points for vehicles and it is vital that those openings are sealed during the voyage. If water does get in, there are few internal bulkheads to prevent it from pouring from side to side along the open space of the vehicle deck. The weight of the water may cause the ship to tip over. That is what happened to the *Herald of Free Enterprise* as it crossed the English Channel in 1987, causing 193 deaths, and to the *Estonia*, which sank in the Baltic Sea in 1994, claiming the lives of 852 people.

TRANSPORTATION

Luxury cruise ships, such as this Caribbean liner, are popular because they combine the comforts of a hotel with mobility.

Sailing for Pleasure

Many people travel by water simply for enjoyment. Recreational sailing is popular on boats ranging from small dinghies to large yachts. Speedboats, also called powerboats, are designed to rise above the water and glide along the surface, enabling them to travel very fast. However, speedboats can pose an environmental threat. They churn up the water and can kill off local plant and animal life. That is a major problem in places such as the Everglades, in Florida, where concern for wildlife, such as the local manatees, has led to increasing restrictions on speed-boating.

Some people like to take their vacations on huge cruise ships, traveling from one place to another. Large ocean liners once dominated passenger transportation across the Atlantic Ocean, but they have since been replaced by planes. Since the 1980s, however, luxury ocean liners have become popular again for cruising. They are like floating hotels, with luxurious facilities for dining, entertainment, and sports.

Water Transportation

 PROS: CRUISE SHIPS

Luxury cruises are popular with many people who want to see the world from a safe base. The tourist trade has become an important source of income for many local economies along cruise routes.

 CONS: CRUISE SHIPS

Infection outbreaks can be a problem on board a cruise ship. Viruses that cause sickness and diarrhea are easily transmitted between passengers living in a relatively enclosed environment.

Cruise ships also release considerable amounts of waste into the sea. Many cruise lines travel similar paths, so their pollution may be harmfully concentrated in specific areas. Those ships also take in and release ballast water. That is water contained in the lower hull to stabilize the ship. Ballast water is often brought on board at one place and discharged in another, introducing foreign organisms, living things that may have a lethal effect on local marine life.

 VIEWPOINT

Environmental Harm From Cruise Ships

Studies have shown that cruise ships produce a lot of pollution relative to their small number of passengers:

"Despite the focus on airline emissions, it has become clear that cruise liners are far more polluting per passenger kilometer than planes."
(Justin Francis, Co-founder of Responsibletravel.com)

"The challenge to ferry companies and cruise lines is to protect the environment, minimize negative impacts ... and support sustainable tourism while meeting the increasing demand for travel."
(Passenger Shipping Association)

21

CHAPTER 3

Rail Travel

In the 19th century, the fastest horse-drawn coaches traveled along Britain's roads at 10 miles per hour (16 kilometers per hour). But in 1829, when a steam-driven locomotive won a competition in northern England, it reached 30 mph (48 kph). The locomotive was the *Rocket,* designed by George Stephenson (see page 6).

By that time, steam engines were already performing many tasks, such as pumping water out of mines and powering factory machinery. Engineers had quickly realized that steam power might also be used to drive a wheeled vehicle. Many worked on developing a locomotive, a mobile steam engine that could pull a train — a chain of linked wagons or carriages — along a fixed track or railway. There had been a number of fairly successful experiments before Stephenson designed the *Rocket,* but his design was the first practical and reliable locomotive.

Steam Locomotives

The command center of a steam locomotive was the cabin, where the engineer and fireman worked. The fireman kept the coal in the firebox burning and stoked. The fire boiled water in a tank that produced steam, which was then forced into cylinders. The pressure of the steam in the cylinder pushed the piston in and out, making the wheels turn. The engineer controlled the locomotive's speed by operating valves that raised or lowered the pressure of steam into and out of the cylinder.

In 1928, the steam engine *Flying Scotsman* made the first nonstop run from London, England to Edinburgh, Scotland.

People hurry through a busy railway station in London. Trains provide vital transportation links in the 21st century.

Trains and railroads were an immediate and spectacular success. By the 1850s, a network of railway lines covered most parts of Britain and other European countries followed suit. The first American railroads were constructed in the 1830s. Railroads were particularly important in the United States because they linked distant places in a vast and still-growing nation. The Union Pacific Railroad was the greatest of several epic American achievements. Completed in 1869, the line stretched across the continent, opening up the American West to new settlements and linking them to established cities in the east.

Steam maintained its supremacy for many years. In the 1930s, Britain produced record-breaking locomotives such as the *Flying Scotsman* and *Mallard*. In 1938, *Mallard* reached a speed of 125 mph (202 kph), which remains the world record for a steam train. In the United States, the most gigantic of all steam locomotives were built in the 1940s. Known as Big Boys, they weighed hundreds of tons, were equipped with 16 huge wheels instead of the standard eight, and were up to 130 feet (40m) long. They hauled very heavy loads over long distances, mastered steep inclines and, during World War II (1939–1945), transported tanks and other military equipment destined for service overseas.

TRANSPORTATION

 PROS: THE COMING OF THE RAILROADS

The railroads had a huge impact on economic growth. They were able to carry large amounts of freight at a time when coal and iron were central to economic development. Railroads enabled millions of people to travel long distances for the first time and gave others a way to commute between home and work.

 CONS: THE COMING OF THE RAILROADS

Steam locomotives produced significant amounts of soot, which added to the coal-based industrial pollution that lasted until the mid-20th century. Rail lines are fixed in place, so other forms of transportation were still needed to take people and goods to and from train stations.

Diesel Trains

An alternative type of engine that ran on a different fuel, diesel, began to replace steam after 1945. The diesel engine is a form of internal combustion engine that uses hot compressed air to ignite the fuel. Some trains use a diesel engine to power the wheels directly, while others use it to power an electric generator that drives motors that turn the wheels. Those diesel-electric trains, particularly favored in the United States and the United Kingdom, are therefore powered by electricity without being dependent on an outside electrical source, such as overhead cables.

Diesel-electric trains are easier to maintain, but are less fuel-efficient than trains powered by diesel engines. Both types are more energy-efficient and cheaper to run than steam trains, and by the 1960s, the United States and Europe had switched to diesel. However, steam trains continue to run in many less economically developed countries.

Burning diesel produces pollutants, including soot and nitrogen oxide, a key ingredient in smog, a fog created by chemical air pollution. Soot and smog have been linked to heart attacks, lung disease, and childhood asthma.

Mountain Climbing

Conventional trains climb steep inclines by winding gradually upward around a hill. Some trains, however, are constructed to go directly up and down a hillside. There are two methods to prevent trains from slipping on the tracks. A rack-and-pinion railway has a third, toothed rail in the middle of the track, called the rack. The train is fitted with a toothed wheel, the pinion, which interlocks continuously with the rack, ensuring the train's safety. A funicular railway has two separate tracks, each fitted with a continuous loop of strong cable laid between the rails. The cable is attached to a train on each track. As the train at the top moves down, its weight hauls the other train up from the bottom.

Switzerland's Jungfrau Railway is the highest in Europe and passes through spectacular alpine scenery. Most of the line operates on the rack-and-pinion principle, in which the train continuously locks in to the "teeth" of the middle rail.

Electric Trains

Many trains are powered directly by electricity. The power for electric trains is supplied either from an overhead cable, or from a third, electrically charged rail line that runs beside the tracks. Those systems work well for short-distance travel within cities, but the cost of electrifying hundreds or thousands of miles of line seemed at first to make them impractical for longer-distance routes. In the late 20th century, however, rising demand for rail services encouraged new investment in long-distance electric lines. Although electrifying rail tracks is very expensive, once it has been done, electric trains are fast and relatively cheap to run.

At first, long-distance electric trains in Europe generally shared the track with other types of rail traffic. However, electric trains that run on tracks specifically designed for them can go much faster. Japanese engineers were the first to design high-speed electric trains with bullet-shaped ends to minimize air resistance. The tracks were made as straight as possible in the interest of speed. In 1964, Japan's "bullet trains" began operating along the Shinkansen line, a 320-mile (515-km) stretch between Tokyo and Osaka. From the beginning, Shinkansen trains achieved speeds of up to 130 mph (210 kph). The Shinkansen was progressively extended and by the 21 century, electric trains were traveling all over Japan on high-speed tracks, reaching top speeds of more than 186 mph (300 kph).

Tilting Trains

A bend in a railroad track forces conventional trains to slow down and therefore lose time. If a conventional train travels at top speed around a bend, the passengers inside feel pushed in the opposite direction and objects slide across the carriage. However, tilting trains can take bends at top speed because they have upper sections that lean. The train actually tilts in the same direction as the bend, just as a racing cyclist leans into a corner. It's more comfortable for passengers too, as nothing slides around the carriage.

Rail Travel

The TGV

Japan still has the fastest regular train services in the world. However, European countries learned from the Japanese example. In 1982, France became the first country in Europe to construct a long-distance line for the exclusive use of high-speed trains. Initially it ran from the capital, Paris, to the southern French city of Lyon. The new type of train was known as the TGV — *train à grande vitesse*, or high-speed train. It is so fast that the driver has no time to see ordinary signals. Instead, instructions reach the driver via electric pulses that pass through the rails.

France's TGV flashes past a field of sunflowers. First introduced in 1982, the TGVs run up to 186 mph (300 kph). A number of other countries have introduced similar services.

TRANSPORTATION

TGV lines have expanded in France and the TGV model has been widely adopted by other countries, including the United Kingdom. In 1994, the Channel Tunnel, a 31-mile (51-km) undersea train tunnel, opened. Passenger and freight trains now run under the English Channel on lines that link the British and French rail systems. In Spain, the Velaro line, running from Madrid to Barcelona, opened in 2008. The Velaro trains average 148 mph (238 kph) and can reach speeds of up to 251mph (404 kph).

Maglev

Magnetic levitation, or maglev, trains use a revolutionary technology that allows them to float above their tracks. A maglev train has no engine or wheels. Instead, it uses electromagnets, powerful magnets operated by an electrical current, to propel itself. Electromagnets are fitted to the bottom of the train and along the tracks, or guideways. The two sets of electromagnets repel each other, lifting the train so that it floats above the guideway. Electromagnetized metal coils on the guideways switch on and off, pushing and pulling the train forward. Because there is no contact between the train and the guideway, and therefore no friction, maglevs are faster, easier to maintain, and quieter than any other type of train currently in service.

Maglev technology was developed in Japan and Germany. A maglev train has already broken the TGV's speed record by reaching 361 mph (581 kph). However, the expense of constructing maglev lines has slowed development, and so far, the only regular service is in Shanghai, China. If the financial problems can be overcome, the maglev may prove to be the passenger train of the future.

VIEWPOINT

Taking Rail to the Next Level

Many people feel that maglev technology represents the future of fast, environmentally friendly transportation:

"Rail has gone as far as it can go. If you want to take it to the next level, you have to go to maglev."

(Phyliss Wilkins, Chairperson of the U.S. Maglev Coalition)

A maglev train in Shanghai, China, glides along its guideway.

Rail Travel

Subway and Light Rail Systems

Moving people around in cities creates special problems for transportation planners. All around the world, huge numbers of workers travel between their homes outside the city and their places of work in the city center. Shoppers and tourists also crowd the world's major cities. All those people want fast and efficient transportation.

Going Underground

In crowded and traffic-jammed cities, one solution is to transport people through tunnels beneath the streets. The world's first underground rail line, the Metropolitan Line in London, opened in 1863. The earliest underground trains were steam-driven, but in the 1890s, electric trains were introduced. Tracks were laid with three rails. The train wheels ran on two of the rails, while the third, electrically charged rail supplied the power. The London Underground was followed by subway, or metro, systems in Budapest, Hungary, in 1896, Boston, Massachusetts, in 1897, and Paris, France, in 1900. Many more were constructed in the 20th century, including New York City's subway system in 1904.

A train pulls into Tottenham Court Road underground station in central London. Where stations are colorfully decorated and well maintained, travel by underground can be pleasant as well as fast and efficient.

TRANSPORTATION

 PROS: UNDERGROUND RAIL SYSTEMS

Although they have existed for more than 100 years, subway systems remain an efficient way for millions of people to move about big cities without interfering with street life or traffic. Like other electric-based systems, subways give off no polluting emissions. During World War II, London Underground stations also served as bomb shelters, protecting civilians during air raids.

 CONS: UNDERGROUND RAIL SYSTEMS

Tunneling and underground construction are extremely expensive. That makes underground systems worth the cost only in big, traffic-jammed cities. Some subway systems are noisy, crowded, hot, and often uncomfortable for their passengers.

Light Rail Systems

The modern tram, or trolley, is a vehicle that carries passengers along rails sunk into city streets. As early as 1853 in Paris, France, horses were used to pull such vehicles. From the 1890s, the vehicles, no longer horse-drawn, were powered by overhead electric wires and competed successfully with motor buses for mass passenger traffic in cities. Some city trains also ran on rails raised above street level. Elevated rail systems, often called "the El," have been in use in New York City since the 1880s and in Chicago since the 1890s.

As car driving became popular, many people viewed trams on fixed rails as obstructive and outdated. In many cities, noisy trams and trains were scrapped

 VIEWPOINT

The Light Rail Solution

Many people are concerned about the problems created by oil-fueled vehicles. Some argue that the best solution is improved public transportation links:

"From an environmental point of view with fuel prices, with climate change, with energy issues, light rail is the answer."

(Catherine Potter, Executive Director of the Regional Conservation Council, campaigning for a light rail system for the Australian capital, Canberra)

between the 1930s and 1950s. More recently, congestion and pollution from cars has changed attitudes. Many cities have installed updated versions of the tram or another light rail system. Those pass through city centers, often in pedestrian areas where cars are not allowed. They may also act as surface extensions of the underground system. For example, the automated Docklands Light Railway opened in 1987 to link the London Underground with the redeveloped areas of East London.

Trains that travel above street level have also made a comeback. Many are monorails, which means they run on a single rail that supplies their electric power. Suspended monorails are particularly spectacular, since they hang below a single rail instead of riding on it.

A modern tram travels on O'Connell Street, the main thoroughfare in the Irish capital, Dublin. Powered by electric cables, trams and other light rail systems are the fastest growing form of urban transportation.

 PROS: LIGHT RAIL SYSTEMS

Light rail systems are efficient, clean, and much less expensive to install than new underground lines. They also reduce car use. A survey carried out in St Louis, Missouri, found that 80 percent of passengers on the city's light rail link preferred it to driving. User-friendly light rail systems have helped to revive many rundown city centers.

CONS: LIGHT RAIL SYSTEMS

Some researchers argue that light rail systems reduce road traffic only temporarily and are not worth the considerable expense involved. Light rail routes, unlike bus routes, are permanent and inflexible. If there is a blockage on the tracks, the trains cannot be diverted around it.

CHAPTER 4

Road Transportation

For thousands of years, people have built roads to make it easier to travel from one place to another. However, roads are expensive to construct and maintain. In the past, empire-builders such as the ancient Romans created large-scale road networks. But when empires fell, roads often decayed into rough paths or disappeared altogether. Modern road systems date back no further than the 18th century. In the last century, they expanded vastly in the developed world as car travel increased. In much of the less developed world there are still few roads and most of the population cannot afford to buy cars.

Mass Production

The first engine-powered road vehicles were developed at the beginning of the 19th century. They were not very practical, however, as the engines constantly needed a constant supply of fresh coal.

The 19th century also saw the introduction of vehicles that ran on electricity. They were more successful, but their range was limited. When their batteries ran out, they took hours to recharge. The breakthrough came in the 1880s, when the first motor cars were fitted with internal combustion engines that ran on gasoline.

At first, driving was an exciting hobby for the few rather than a revolutionary new mode of transportation. The age of the car really began

The Bicycle

Bicycles became popular in the 1880s, when the first practical models were developed. Today, many countries promote bicycle use for environmental reasons. A bicycle requires no fuel. Its power comes from its rider, who pushes two pedals to turn the wheels via a connecting chain. Cycling gives off no harmful emissions, creates no noise pollution, and is great exercise. In parts of the developing world, cycling is the main form of transportation.

after 1908, when Henry Ford introduced mass-production techniques at his factory in Detroit, Michigan. Initially, Ford made a single standardized type of car, the Ford Model-T. The Model-T was the first widely affordable car. In the next few decades, other companies followed Ford's example. Competition between manufacturers, along with new technologies, helped to push down prices, enabling more and more people to buy their own cars. Mechanized road transportation developed rapidly, replacing horseback riding and horse-drawn vehicles.

The availability of cars has fundamentally affected everyday life in the developed world. Settlement patterns changed, since people no longer needed to live near the places where they worked and shopped. They could move far away from the city to surrounding suburbs, or even farther away to remote areas and drive to work or to the supermarket.

Robotic arms make sparks fly as they work on a car production line in Beijing, China. Advanced methods of mass production helped make cars widely affordable in the 20th century. Today, automation makes mass production easier than ever.

TRANSPORTATION

 PROS: VEHICLES TODAY

Cheap, mass-produced road vehicles have given people the freedom of movement. People can travel by car whenever they choose, without being limited by public transportation schedules. Many people may prefer to travel in their cars because of the greater comfort, privacy, and convenience they offer.

Road vehicles also have great economic importance. Commuters can travel long distances to work by car, opening up a wider choice of job opportunities. Businesses can distribute their goods quickly, efficiently, and cheaply. Most long-distance cargo spends some part of its journey in a road vehicle. Trucks are not limited to traveling on fixed rails or between ports or airports, so they can carry products and materials from door to door.

 CONS: VEHICLES TODAY

The billions of vehicles on the world's roads produce huge amounts of pollution and the oil that fuels them is a non-renewable resource. In spite of that, many people buy cars that make very inefficient use of fuel. Particularly notorious examples of those vehicles, often described as "gas guzzlers," are sport utility vehicles (SUVs). The ever-increasing use of the car means that many roads are choked with traffic. The construction of new roads, often undertaken to ease congestion, has destroyed large areas of countryside. Other solutions for reducing traffic, such as making drivers pay tolls or charges for using busy roads, are generally unpopular.

Cleaner Engines

World demand for oil is enormous. That is partly a result of the tremendous expansion of car use, although other forms of transportation also make heavy use of oil products such as gasoline and diesel. The Earth's oil reserves are limited, so in the coming decades it will become increasingly difficult to find new supplies of oil. One day, it will all be gone.

Trucks and cars drive on an interstate highway in the United States. Road links are essential for the delivery of long-distance cargo.

In recent years, many people have accepted that something must be done to reduce our dependence on oil. But few people are ready to give up the freedom brought by the car. The ideal solution is to replace oil with a different, cleaner, renewable fuel.

Catalytic Converters

The development of the catalytic converter was an important advancement in reducing emissions from gasoline engines. Catalytic converters work by collecting the exhaust fumes produced by the engine and changing their chemical composition. The converters change the poisonous gases nitrous oxide and carbon monoxide into other gases. However, the catalytic converter does not reduce carbon dioxide emissions, so it does not change the contribution made by car use to climate change (see page 8).

TRANSPORTATION

Currently, one of the most promising alternative technologies is the hybrid car. Hybrid cars use both an internal combustion engine and an electric motor. That is called dual-engine technology. Hybrid vehicles use the electric motor at low power levels and the gasoline engine when more power is needed. The electric battery is charged by the motion of the car when it is running on gasoline. That means a hybrid can run mostly off its batteries when moving slowly, for example in busy city traffic, but switches to its internal combustion engine for high-speed driving. Some of the earliest and most successful hybrids were the Toyota Prius, which was first sold in 1997, and the Honda Insight, released in 1999. Today there are a number of hybrid models on the market.

Hybrids use less oil, so they produce fewer emissions than ordinary cars. They are not the final solution to oil dependence, as they still use some oil and emit pollutants, but they are a step in the right direction. The future may belong to cars that do not use internal combustion engines at all, but instead run on electricity produced by a "clean" source such as solar power or hydrogen fuel cells (see page 57).

PROS: HYBRID CARS

Hybrid cars burn less oil than conventional cars do, so they produce less emissions. Since they use nonpolluting electric power when traveling at low speeds, hybrid cars help reduce pollution in congested cities. Hybrid cars also reduce noise pollution, because they are very quiet when running on electric motors. Because they use less fuel, hybrid cars cost less to run than vehicles that use gasoline.

CONS: HYBRID CARS

Hybrid cars are more expensive than conventional cars because their engines are more complicated to make. They need more electrical systems and more batteries than vehicles that run on only one fuel source. Cars have a long operational life, so even if new customers buy hybrids, there will be many old cars on the road for years to come.

A hybrid electric bus travels along Broadway in New York City. Such buses help reduce polluting emissions and use less fuel than conventional vehicles.

Preparing for Life Without Oil

VIEWPOINT

Many experts argue that we must investigate a range of alternative fuel options:

"No single technology development or alternative fuel can solve the problems of growing transportation fuel use and ... emissions. Progress must come from a comprehensive, coordinated effort to develop and market more efficient vehicles and benign fuels, and to find more sustainable ways to satisfy transportation demands."

(Massachusetts Institute of Technology report on reducing fuel use and emissions)

TRANSPORTATION

Biofuels

Biofuels offer an alternative to fossil fuels. Biofuels are made from carbon extracted from biomass, biological material such as corn, rapeseed, soybeans, or sugar cane. Unlike fossil fuels, biofuels are renewable as new crops can be grown each year. Burning biofuels is also "carbon neutral," meaning that it does not add to the amount of carbon dioxide (CO_2) in Earth's atmosphere. Burning biofuel does produce CO_2, but it releases the same amount of carbon dioxide that the plant absorbed while it was growing. Though current vehicles do not usually run exclusively on biofuels, many countries are already mixing biofuels with fossil fuels. Brazil is the largest exporter of a biofuel called ethanol and is regarded as a world leader in biofuels. Since 1976, ethanol made from sugar cane has, by law, been mixed into all of the gasoline sold in Brazil.

VIEWPOINT

The Way Ahead?

Biofuel production raises both environmental and social issues. Supporters remain optimistic about using it to meet future energy needs. Others warn that, if not carefully managed, biofuel production could have negative impacts on people and the environment:

"[Biofuels are] an opportunity to add to the world supply of energy to meet the enormous growing demand and hopefully to mitigate [lessen] some of the price effects [of rising energy costs]. It's an opportunity to do so in an environmentally friendly way and in a way that is carbon neutral. It's an opportunity to do so in a way that developing countries like Brazil can provide income and employment for their people."
(Paul Wolfowitz, Former President of the World Bank)

"Liquid biofuel production could threaten the availability of adequate food supplies by diverting land and other productive resources away from food crops."
(United Nations report Sustainable Bioenergy, 2007)

Corn is unloaded for processing into ethanol biofuel at a plant in Iowa. Ethanol production is a controversial issue because it makes use of agricultural land that could be used for food production.

 PROS: BIOFUELS

Mixing some biofuels into gasoline and diesel reduces the consumption of those oil-based fuels. The more biofuels are used, the longer the world's supply of oil will last. As fossil fuels become more scarce, biofuels may provide a less expensive alternative.

 CONS: BIOFUELS

Burning biofuels is carbon neutral, but producing biofuels uses a lot of energy. Oil and electricity are needed to grow, harvest, process, and transport the biofuel. Biofuel production also requires large areas of land and a supply of water to grow the plants. In some countries, farmers can make more money growing crops for biofuels than food crops. That has led to a drop in the production of some food crops and a rise in world food prices. The increasing demand for biofuels could also be a threat to the world's rain forests. The destruction of rain forests to make room for biofuel crops could accelerate if the demand for biofuels continues.

TRANSPORTATION

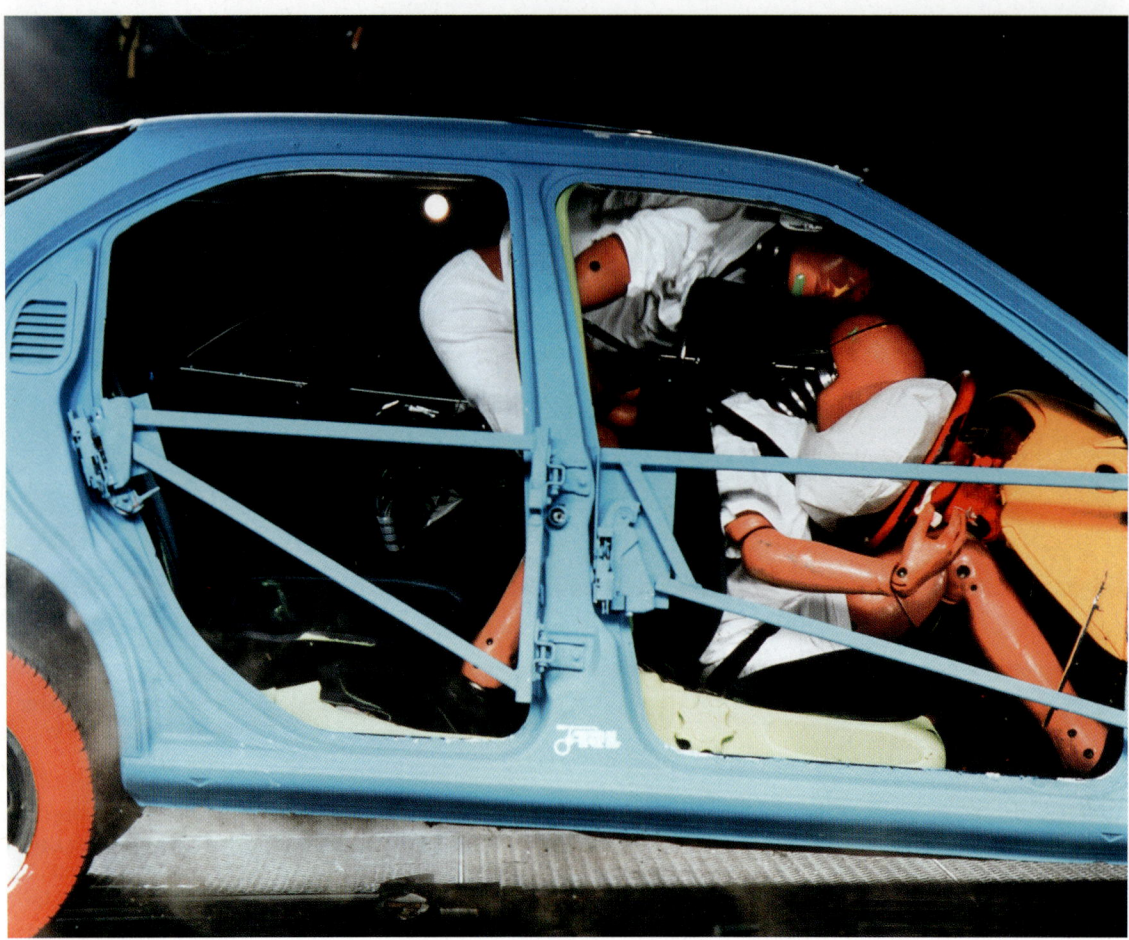

Safety First

Scientists and engineers have made many technological improvements since the early days of Ford's Model-T. Today, modern cars use a variety of safety systems to limit the severity of a crash. Seat belts began to appear in cars in the 1950s. Seat belts have mechanisms that tighten the belt when it is pulled hard and fast, as it would be during a crash. Fixed to the body of the car, a seat belt prevents the wearer from being thrown about violently in a collision. Another safety device, the airbag, has been built into some cars since the 1970s. At first those inflatable cushions were installed on the driver's side only, but many modern cars have them for passengers, too. If there is a crash, a sensor triggers the airbag to inflate in a fraction of a second. Airbags help reduce injuries by preventing people from slamming into the hard parts of the vehicle's interior.

Analysis of crash tests helps experts improve car safety. Using dummies in the tests gives experts an idea of how humans will be affected, but avoids putting lives at risk.

Engineers carry out extensive tests to establish the effects of different impacts on the vehicle. They simulate different accidents using dummies in the place of real passengers. That is called crash testing and it has helped engineers develop designs that help protect passengers. For example, the front of many vehicles is designed to crush easily on impact. Called the crumple zone, it functions as a buffer, absorbing the shock of an impact to lessen the effect an accident would have on people inside the car.

Such safety features have greatly increased the chances of surviving a crash. However, although the percentage of accidents resulting in deaths is down, the overall number of deaths continues to grow as traffic volumes increase.

ABS Brakes

Modern cars include devices that give the driver improved control over the vehicle. For instance, an antilock braking system (ABS) is designed to help drivers maintain control of a vehicle if they have to brake suddenly. It takes a wheel less time to stop turning than it takes a moving car to stop. If one wheel locks up when a driver brakes, the car is likely to spin, skid, or even flip over. ABS prevents any of the wheels on a car from locking up. Computerized sensors on each wheel report the speed of the wheel to the ABS control unit. A wheel that is rotating more slowly than the others is beginning to lock. The ABS system fixes the problem by automatically adjusting the braking pressure on that wheel, enabling a driver to steer more effectively while braking.

A car lies on its roof after a road accident. Luckily, the driver survived.

TRANSPORTATION

Speeding

Driving above the legal speed limit is a major cause of road accidents. Science and technology have been used to tackle speeding in several ways. Speed cameras are used to photograph drivers who break the law, so that police can identify and fine them. Another simple but effective technology is the speed bump. That is a raised section in the road that forces a driver to slow down or risk damage to the car's suspension.

Other new technologies help drivers obey the law. Cruise control systems, for example, can be used to maintain a steady speed on long stretches of road. More sophisticated automated systems, called Advanced Driver Assistance Systems (ADAS), help drivers control their cars. Some modern cars are fitted with adaptive cruise control. That system uses lasers or radar to monitor the distance between the car and the vehicle ahead. It slows the car down when it detects the vehicle in front getting too close and speeds up again when it is safe to do so. There are several types of ADAS, performing tasks ranging from helping drivers find their way to their destinations to detecting that they are falling asleep at the wheel and alerting them.

A handheld speed camera, one of the modern technologies that help police catch drivers who break the speed limit, tracks drivers on a highway.

PROS: TECHNOLOGY TO THE RESCUE

Studies have consistently shown that safety systems, such as seat belts and airbags, improve accident survival rates. Technologies that help drivers respect speed limits are also likely to reduce the number of accidents. That approach may be more successful than punishing people by fining them.

 CONS: TECHNOLOGY TO THE RESCUE

Seat belts and airbags do occasionally injure people. Airbags inflate very fast and can be particularly dangerous to children sitting in the front seat if they hit them in the head. For that reason, young children should sit in the back of a car in correctly fitted car seats.

Systems such as cruise control reduce the driver's activity and may cause the driver to lose concentration or fall asleep. Such outcomes could actually cause accidents. Some people think control systems make machines the masters of people. Not everyone trusts computers with their safety.

 VIEWPOINT

Driver Assistance Systems

Many people think that increased automation would significantly reduce car accidents:

"Studies show that at least 93 percent of accidents are caused by human error, so the case for increased driver assistance is clear .... By decreasing the driver's workload, detecting dangers, and providing the necessary support in hazardous situations, Advanced Driver Assistance Systems (ADAS) could save a considerable number of lives every year."

(Michael Nielsen, Director for Development and Deployment for ERTICO–ITS, a group that specializes in intelligent transportation systems)

CHAPTER 5

Air Travel

People have long dreamed of traveling through the air. Even ancient myths told stories of individuals who, according to legend, flew using their arm muscles to move bird-like wings. From the late 18th century, aeronauts, or air travelers, rose into the sky in hot-air or gas-filled balloons. A successful attempt to make a heavier-than-air craft took much longer to achieve. Finally, two brothers, Orville and Wilbur Wright, designed and built a wooden plane with two sets of wings. They tested the biplane, *Flyer*, on December 17, 1903, at Kitty Hawk, North Carolina. Piloted by Orville, *Flyer* traveled 121 feet (37 meters). The flight lasted only 12 seconds, but it began the real conquest of air travel.

Within a few years, aviation was headline news. When Louis Blériot made the first flight across the English Channel in 1909, people began to realize that flying would change the future of travel. The outbreak of World War I (1914–1918) sped up technological innovation. Metal was used to build planes instead of wood, and planes with a single set of wings, called monoplanes, began to replace biplanes. Many heroic record-breaking flights were made during the 1920s and 1930s. The most famous was Charles Lindbergh's solo nonstop flight across the Atlantic Ocean from New York to Paris in 1927. Commercial airlines began passenger services, although they were able to carry only a handful of people on each flight. Planes carried some freight, notably

Taking to the Air

The design of an aircraft's wings gives the "lift" needed to rise into the air. The upper surface of the wings is slightly curved and the undersurface is close to flat. When the plane is moving at a sufficient speed, air passing over the curved surface moves more quickly than air passing along the flatter surface. Since fast-moving air exerts less pressure than slow-moving air, the air under the wings pushes upward, lifting the plane.

mail. Mail planes, seaplanes, and light aircraft such as those used by "flying doctors" in Australia, brought many small, remote communities into contact with the wider world.

World War II (1939–1945) further advanced aircraft technology. Larger planes were developed to carry troops and huge quantities of freight. Those would become models for large passenger airliners and commercial transportation planes. The most striking feature of air warfare, however, was the bombing of cities on a scale never seen before. The German "Blitz" of Britain and the devastating bombing of Germany by the Allies destroyed both military and civilian targets. In 1945, the United States used bomber planes to drop two atomic bombs that wiped out the Japanese cities Hiroshima and Nagasaki.

Piloted by Captain Charles Lindbergh, the *Spirit of St. Louis* takes off from Roosevelt Field in New York, on May 20, 1927. Lindbergh went on to complete the first solo flight across the Atlantic Ocean, landing at Le Bourget, Paris, on the following day.

TRANSPORTATION

 PROS: EARLY AIRCRAFT IN PEACE AND WAR

Early feats of aviation were sensational, but their impact on ordinary society was limited. However, flights to and from remote communities improved global links in a way that would continue into the 21st century. During an international crisis in 1938, the British Prime Minister, Neville Chamberlain, twice flew to Germany for talks with the German dictator Adolf Hitler. That was an early example of a new kind of leader-to-leader political negotiation that would later become common.

 CONS: EARLY AIRCRAFT IN PEACE AND WAR

Aircraft played an increasingly important role in both world wars. The suffering of civilian populations under massive bombing raids was a new development in the history of war. It meant that conflicts involved entire peoples, not just the armed forces.

The Jet Age

Work on the jet engine began in the 1930s and continued during World War II. Traveling at more than 596 mph (960 kph), even the earliest jets moved twice as fast as propeller-driven planes. After the end of World War II, jet engines were developed to power military aircraft. Then, in 1952, the British company de Havilland put the first jet airliner into service. In 1970, the American company Boeing introduced the 747, the first wide-bodied "jumbo jet." It was the world's largest passenger aircraft and would eventually be capable of carrying

The Jet Engine

A jet engine works by sucking in air through its spinning front blades and compressing it so that the air moves with tremendous force. The air passes into a combustion chamber, where it is mixed with liquid fuel. An electric spark ignites the air and fuel mixture. It expands into a burning gas and is blasted out of the nozzle or rear jet. This hurls the plane forward at an incredible speed. Most modern jet engines, called turbofans, blow air around as well as through the engine. That diminishes engine noise and strengthens the airflow, further increasing the turbofan's power.

An Airbus 380 lands at the Paris Air Show in 2007. This huge aircraft can carry up to 500 people in great comfort. First-class passengers enjoy luxuries such as private meeting rooms.

more than 400 passengers. In 1974, the European-based Airbus entered service and soon competed strongly with Boeing.

Jet airliners went into service at a time when many countries in North America and Western Europe were becoming more prosperous. People were able to afford luxury vacations, and jet airliners made it possible for many people to travel abroad for the first time. Competition between companies kept prices low. As a result, mass tourism became one of the major industries of modern times.

Many people now believe that the continuing expansion of air travel is having a negative impact on the world. Aircraft engines emit huge quantities of the greenhouse gas carbon dioxide, while emissions of nitrogen oxide cause air pollution around airports. There are also serious problems with noise pollution along flight paths near airports. There are proposals to tax the air travel industry to help pay for the environmental damage it causes. One reason why mass air travel is so popular is that there is no tax on aviation fuel used for international flights. That makes flying less expensive than many other forms of transportation. Because of international agreements, that situation is hard to change, though many governments now levy taxes on individual ticket-holders.

TRANSPORTATION

 PROS: MASS AIR TRAVEL

Large numbers of people now enjoy experiences that formerly only the rich could afford. Tourism stimulates the world economy and brings money and employment to poor countries visited by wealthy tourists. Air travel has helped many businesses expand globally. Businesspeople routinely fly to corporate offices all over the world for meetings and to check in on operations in other countries.

 CONS: MASS AIR TRAVEL

Planes are among the worst polluters, responsible for more than half the environmental damage done by all forms of transportation. Low aviation taxes are unfair to competing forms of transportation, including more environmentally friendly services, such as trains. Worldwide air travel has also had an impact on health. Travelers who move rapidly from one continent to another can spread infectious diseases with frightening speed. That happened in 2003, when a new disease called SARS (severe acute respiratory syndrome) spread within a few months from China to places all over the world.

 VIEWPOINT

Greenhouse Guilt

Environmental organizations such as Friends of the Earth are critical of the United Kingdom's policies on climate change and the role of aviation. In 2007, a spokesperson declared that:

"Aviation is the fastest growing source of carbon dioxide in the United Kingdom. Emissions have more than doubled since 1990. The government must ensure the cost of flying reflects the environmental damage aviation causes. And it should abandon plans to allow new runways to be built."

(Mike Childs, Senior Campaigner, Friends of the Earth)

Supersonic Flight

Flight is supersonic when it is faster than the speed at which sound travels, which is about 761 mph (1,226 kph). When an aircraft reaches that speed, it is said to have broken the sound barrier. Supersonic military jets began flying in 1947. The United Kingdom and France cooperated to produce Concorde, which in 1976 became the first supersonic passenger airliner to go into regular service. With its beak-like nose and wings, Concorde became world famous. Cruising at an average speed of 1,336 mph (2,150 kph), Concorde could carry 100 passengers from New York to London in just three-and-a-half hours. That is half the time it takes a normal jet to cross the Atlantic Ocean. Concorde broke many speed records before being retired in 2003. Because of their great expense, no more supersonic airliners have since been built.

Passengers wear masks on a 2003 flight from Manilla, in the Philippines, to Singapore. The masks are protection against SARS, a dangerous flu-like illness that was carried by air travelers and rapidly spread across the world.

TRANSPORTATION

An Antonov 225 cargo plane takes off from Frankfurt-Hahn Airport in Germany. The world's largest operational aircraft, the six-engined Russian Antonov was originally designed to carry parts for the Soviet space program.

Transporting Cargo by Air

Most passenger aircraft carry some freight, but much greater amounts are transported by specialized cargo planes. Since the 1960s, consumers in prosperous countries have bought goods that are manufactured or produced abroad, often on other

Space Transportation

Space vehicles are probably the most exclusive forms of transportation. In 1961, Yuri Gagarin, a Russian, became the first person in space, orbiting Earth in *Vostok 1*. Yet even now, only about 500 people have gone into space. They include the teams of the U.S. Apollo missions, which included in the landing of *Apollo 11* on the Moon in 1969. Early rocket-powered spacecraft could be used only once. Today, astronauts travel to and from the International Space Station aboard the space shuttle. The shuttle is designed to land like an airplane and can be reused again and again.

continents. That globalization of trade means that many goods are transported thousands of miles across the world to be sold. In wealthy countries, many consumers have acquired a taste for exotic or out-of-season foods. Air transportation is a good way to carry perishable food, such as fruit and fish, because it is much faster than sea or road transportation.

The cargo plane has become a specialized aircraft. It is big-bodied, with wings and tail mounted high to make loading and unloading cargoes as easy as possible. Cargo planes can carry heavy loads but supercargo planes have an astonishing capacity. The largest supercargo plane is the gigantic, six-engined Antonov 225, which can fly up to 500 mph (800 kph) and carry cargo weighing up to 551,155 pounds (250,000 kilograms). It can hold another plane or a locomotive, but on its first commercial flight in 2002, it transported 216,000 prepared meals from Stuttgart, Germany, to Oman for U.S. military personnel.

PROS: AIR FREIGHT

The goods transported by cargo planes offer people a wider range of things to buy. Cargo planes make it possible for fresh produce to be exported to countries all over the world. This benefits the global economy and increases trade opportunities between poor and rich countries. When a disaster occurs, cargo planes can bring emergency medical and food supplies to remote places.

CONS: AIR FREIGHT

Like passenger aircraft, freight planes are a major source of pollution. That may prove to be too high an environmental price to pay for the luxury of transporting exotic foods around the world. Globalization has significant disadvantages. In practice, many food-producing countries have specialized in growing particular crops to supply wealthy countries and then found themselves at the mercy of changes in demand.

CHAPTER 6

Future Transportation

It is hard to predict what transportation will be like in the future. No one can be certain what forms the next great breakthroughs will take. Some people believe there will be intergalactic spacecraft and energy beams that instantly transport a person from one place to another. Those remain science fiction, at least for the time being. But new developments in water, rail, road, and air travel may be just around the corner.

Faster Sea Travel

Despite the role played by supertankers, sea travel is less important today than it was a century ago. Slower than aircraft and less convenient than cars, ships face competition. But innovations in water transportation could change the future.

New technologies may enable engineers to build much faster seafaring vehicles. One example is the supersonic submarine. Scientists and engineers have already broken the underwater sound barrier using small test models. No one has built an operational supersonic submarine yet, but such a vessel could potentially achieve incredible speeds — thanks to a bubble of gas!

The key to that technology is to insulate the object from the water around it. Water is

Air Lubrication

Under development by the Maritime Research Institute Netherlands (MARIN), air lubrication seems likely to be widely used long before the supersonic submarine. The idea is to create a layer of gas between the hull of the ship and the water, reducing friction between the two. Researchers have had some success testing this method on small model craft, but it has yet to be tried on full-size ships. Air lubrication could substantially reduce fuel consumption and, therefore, the running costs and environmental impact of seafaring.

much denser than air, so it produces far more resistance to the progress of a craft. Insulating a submarine by surrounding it with a gas bubble reduces resistance and allows the craft to move faster. However, scientists have not yet found a way to sustain supersonic speeds over a long period undersea. Propelling a full-size supersonic submarine would require a great deal of thrust. Existing engines that are powerful enough for the task are too large and heavy to be outfitted for a submarine. If engineers overcome those difficulties, the supersonic submarine could have a promising future.

This artist's impression contrasts a normal submarine (*top*) with a supersonic submarine surrounded by a bubble of gas. The bubble does away with the drag caused by the contact between the water and the submarine's surface, which slows down present-day vessels.

PROS: SUPERSONIC SUBMARINE

Undersea travel could provide low-cost and low-pollution transportation. It could also reduce people's current dependence on air travel. In the future, perhaps people will go to their vacation destinations aboard supersonic submarines.

CONS: SUPERSONIC SUBMARINE

Opening up the undersea environment to increased human travel could have an unfavorable impact on marine life. A submarine may discharge pollutants into the surrounding water. The high-speed passage of a supersonic submarine might also have unforeseen effects on underwater life.

TRANSPORTATION

Flying Trains

Kohama Laboratory at Tohoku University, Japan, is developing a new transportation technology that merges air and rail travel. The aero-train hovers about a third of an inch (1 centimeter) above its track. It has L-shaped wings that enable it to ride on a pocket of high-pressure air within a walled track. The aero-train's greatest advantage is its low energy consumption. It is a clean form of rail transportation that runs on solar and wind power. Designers hope to have a full-scale train, capable of traveling up to 217 mph (350 kph), running by 2020.

The aero-train will have a walled track to enable it to fly along a pocket of trapped air. It will be powered entirely by clean sources, including wind power captured by turbines.

High-Tech Railways

Some modern trains are impressively fast, but new technology could increase speeds even further. One idea for the future is the vacuum tube train. The air around us on Earth contains molecules of gas but they are not present in a vacuum — it is completely empty space. That means an object can travel at extremely high speeds through a vacuum, because there is no air resistance.

Vacuum tube trains would work on the maglev principle (page 28). But as well as hovering above magnetized rails, they would travel through a system of large tubes. The air would be sucked out to create a vacuum inside the tubes, allowing the train to travel through them at incredible speeds. Engineers think that a vacuum tube train might achieve speeds as fast as 1,988 mph (3,200 kph). The trains would be designed so that cars could be driven on to them at local stations. One idea is to construct a submerged floating tube about 150 to 300 feet (45 to 90 meters) beneath the Atlantic Ocean, anchored at intervals to the ocean bed. Trains inside the tube would be able to cover the distance between the United States and Europe in an hour. With a worldwide network of vacuum tubes, global travel could become amazingly fast.

PROS: VACUUM TUBE TRAINS

Vacuum tube trains could provide fast transportation around the world. They would run on electricity, preferably generated using clean technologies. That could lead to a reduction in pollution by reducing the number of air and road journeys. If people were able to drive their cars onto the vacuum tube train, they could travel conveniently to and from stations. By taking the train for part of the trip, they would make their journey faster and create less pollution.

CONS: VACUUM TUBE TRAINS

Building a network of vacuum tubes would be hugely expensive. It would require a massive investment by private companies or nations. People would probably object to the ugliness of giant tubes unless they were built underground or along the seabed. Wherever the tubes were located, clearing a path for them would have a powerful and probably undesirable impact on the natural environment.

Many people have tried to develop flying cars. This artist's drawing shows the Moller Skycar, which has been in development since the 1960s. How well it will perform is still not fully known.

Fueling the Future

For the last two centuries, the main forms of transportation have depended on burning fossil fuels. But now the threat of climate change and the eventual exhaustion of oil reserves make it vital for people to develop different, sustainable energy sources.

Electricity could become an unlimited source of power for cars. Today, electric cars have a limited range because their batteries soon run out and take a long time to

Flying Cars

Cars that could fly seem like a sci-fi dream that would make traffic jams a thing of the past! However, a British company, Parajet, has developed the Skycar, a buggy fitted with an unfolding wing which drivers can deploy when they wish to take to the skies. A powerful rear fan provides the lift that carries the Skycar up and away, at speeds of up to 80 mph (130 kph). Even so, it could be some years before most of us are capable of traveling to work or school in our flying cars!

recharge. Using hydrogen fuel cells would be one way of solving that problem. The hydrogen is extracted from water in a process called electrolysis and used to power hydrogen fuel cells. A hydrogen vehicle can use this fuel to produce electricity by converting the hydrogen back into water. Instead of being plugged in for hours to recharge its batteries, a hydrogen vehicle can refill at a hydrogen fueling station. Some hydrogen cars and fueling stations already exist, but the technology is not yet widely available. It remains to be seen whether this or other alternatives will power the cars of the future.

PROS: HYDROGEN CARS

Hydrogen cars may be the solution to the problems of 21st-century road transportation. Hydrogen is produced from water, which is far more abundant than the oil used to produce gas. The water is not lost in the process, but re-formed as a by-product of releasing the energy from the hydrogen. The process of generating electricity from a hydrogen cell also produces no pollution. The hydrogen-fueled car's only emission is water vapor.

CONS: HYDROGEN CARS

If hydrogen-fueled cars became popular, a vast and expensive network of hydrogen refueling stations would have to be constructed. Vehicles that burn hydrogen do not produce pollutants, but they are environmentally friendly only if the hydrogen fuel cells are manufactured in a clean way. To make the fuel cells, electricity is used to extract hydrogen from water. But much of today's electricity is produced by burning fossil fuels, the resources we hope to do without! To be a real advancement, the fuel cells for hydrogen vehicles would have to be manufactured using alternative sources of electricity, such as nuclear, wind, or solar power. It may be better to focus on improving battery design, so that cars can run directly on electricity rather than making it from hydrogen.

TRANSPORTATION

This illustration shows two passenger shuttles docking at a space hotel, with the International Space Station visible in the distance. Space tourism might become common during the 21st century.

Transportation Above and Beyond

The future will bring faster, better, and cleaner versions of existing forms of transportation: new ships, trains, cars, and planes. But it may also radically change where and how we travel. A limited number of individuals — mostly scientists and highly trained astronauts — have already traveled into space, reaching as far as the Moon. However, services offering to take paying customers up into space are already running. "Space tourism" may prove to be the beginning of mass travel, or even settlement, in space.

 PROS: SPACE PLANES

Traveling into space could mark the beginning of a new era for humanity. Astronauts have described how wonderful it is to see Earth from space. In the near future, many more people may experience this. Space transportation could open up new possibilities for the human race, such as the colonization of other planets and the mining of resources on moons and asteroids.

 CONS: SPACE PLANES

Regular launches of space planes into orbit involve burning massive quantities of fuel that damages the environment. Future technologies may help to minimize that damage, but traveling into space is likely to remain very expensive in terms of money and resources.

Future of Transportation

VIEWPOINT

Everyone seems to be worried about pollution, congestion, and the exhaustion of fossil fuels. But some people are optimistic about the future of transportation:

"In a relatively short period of time — maybe 15 to 20 years — I believe we're going to fly hypersonic [more than five times faster than the speed of sound] .... Travel time may be reduced to as little as 60 minutes anywhere on Earth."

(Burt Rutan, Aerospace Engineer and Designer of SpaceShipOne, the first privately-developed crewed vessel to reach space)

GLOSSARY

aviation The art and science of flying aircraft

ballast tank A tank on a boat or ship that is filled with water to help keep the craft stable; in submarines, the ballast tank is filled or emptied to enable the vessel to rise or dive

ballast water The water used to fill a ballast tank

biofuel Fuel made from biomass, usually plants

biomass Organic matter such as plants or animals

bulk cargo Cargo, usually raw materials or food, that is carried loose

bulkhead A partition on a boat, separating different sections

carbon A nonmetallic chemical element that combines with other elements to form the basis of living organisms

carbon neutral Not emitting carbon, or compensating for carbon emitted by absorbing an equal amount of carbon

cargo Goods carried by commercial transportation

catamaran A vessel with two hulls

climate change A term that describes any change in climate, but typically the temperature changes believed to be taking place in the world's climate as a result of burning fossil fuels

compressed Describes a substance that has been pressed or squeezed so that it occupies less space

container ship A ship designed to carry cargo in standard-sized containers

crash test A test carried out on a vehicle, using dummies instead of human passengers, that is designed to establish the effect of different impacts on the vehicle

cruise control An automated system that controls the speed at which a vehicle moves

crumple zone The front part of a vehicle that is designed to cushion the passenger compartment in the event of a crash

domestication The adaptation of a plant or animal so that humans can make use of it

double hulled Describes a ship with an inner and an outer hull

electrolysis The passing of electricity through a liquid in order to separate it into its component parts; the process used to separate water (hydrogen oxide) into hydrogen and oxygen

electromagnet A magnet that produces a magnetic field only when an electric current is passed through it

emission Gas that is sent out or discharged when fossil fuels are burned; more widely, any gas, fluid, or heat that is given off

fossil fuel A fuel, such as oil, natural gas, or coal, that is made up of the decomposed remains of plant and animals

freight Goods carried by commercial transportation

friction The resistance caused by the rubbing together of two objects that are in contact and which can slow down vehicles, such as resistance between the wheels and tracks slows down a train

fuel cell A mechanism that produces energy by combining elements to create a reaction; in most fuel cells, hydrogen is combined with oxygen to release energy and water

funicular A type of mountain railway with two cars attached to a continous loop of cable and one that uses the weight of the downward car to pull the other car up the mountain

gasoline A form of fuel made from oil and used in internal combustion engines

generator A device for generating electricity

global warming The process by which the average temperatures of the near-Earth atmosphere and Earth's surface are gradually rising

greenhouse gas Any gas that contributes to climate change by retaining heat from the Sun in Earth's atmosphere

hovercraft A craft, usually used as a ferry, that moves above water on a cushion of air

hull The main body of a vessel

hybrid Something that combines two different types of things, such as a hybrid car, which runs on two different power sources

hydrofoil A craft that moves above water, carried by a streamlined, wing-shaped structure, called a foil

Industrial Revolution A period that began in the late 18th century in Britain in which there was rapid development of industrial technology and the use of energy from fossil fuels

internal combustion engine The type of engine used in cars, based on the continuous combustion (burning) of gasoline

lock On a canal, a device that enables boats to move up or down from one level to another

locomotive The engine used to draw a train along a track

maglev A high-speed train, raised in the air by magnetism so that it floats above the rails

mass production An industrial technique by which goods are produced in huge quantities through standardization, each item being identical

merchant ship A ship used in commerce

navigation The art and science of planning and following a route to reach a specific destination

paddle boat A boat that is propelled by paddle wheels, either at the back or on each side

piston A movable rod or disc in steam and other engines

Plimsoll line The line on the hull of a ship that indicates how low in the water it can sit, and therefore the maximum load for that ship

Per passenger kilometer A unit of measure representing the transportation of one passenger over a distance of one kilometer; per passenger kilometers are calculated by multipying the number of passengers by the distance traveled

propeller A device with blades radiating from a hub

GLOSSARY

rack-and-pinion Describes a type of mountain railway in which a toothed wheel (the pinion) continuously locks the train to a central toothed rail (the rack)

roll-on roll-off (ro-ro) A type of ferry with doors at either end to allow vehicles to drive on and off in the same direction

sensor A device that detects changes in its environment, such as to trigger the inflation of an airbag when it registers the impact of a car crash

ship canal A canal that links two seas or oceans, or one that links a port to the coast

single hulled Describes a ship with one hull

sluice gate In the lock gate of a canal, a small panel that allows water to enter or leave the lock

smog A chemical fog

smuggle To import or export something illegally and secretly

solar power Energy from the Sun

soot Powdery black matter, deposited on surroundings after substances such as coal have been burned

spoke On a wheel, one of the bars that connects the hub (center) and the rim, holding the rim firmly in place

supersonic Faster than the speed of sound (about 780 mph or 1,255 kph)

TGV (*train à grande vitesse*) One of the fleet of high-speed trains that forms part of the rail network in France

thrust A force that produces motion, for example from the movement of a propeller

vacuum Empty space containing no matter, not even air

valve A device that regulates the flow of gas or liquid in machinery by opening or shutting

wind power Energy produced by harnessing the force of the wind

FURTHER INFORMATION

WEB SITES

Chicago History Museum
www.chicagohs.org/education/resources/hands/transportation-history
The Chicago History Museum web site features downloadable information for students about modes of transportation throughout history.

Ecokids.com
www.ecokids.ca/pub/eco_info/topics/environmental/errandRun/index.cfm
This interactive game from Ecokids.com shows how alternative methods of transportation can help protect the environment.

TransitPeople's Transportation Lessons
www.transitpeople.org/lesson/trancovr.htm
TransitPeople's Transportation Lessons web site covers transportation history, examines problems caused by cars, and describes different modes of public transportation, including trains.

Transportation in Japan
www.transport-pf.or.jp/english/index.html
The Transportation in Japan site has information about Japanese transportation history and vehicles of all kinds. It includes online activities and suggestions for further investigation.

U.S. Energy Information Administration
www.eia.doe.gov/kids/history/timelines/transportation.html
The student section of the U.S. Energy Information Administration web site includes a time line about important milestones in U.S. transportation history.

U.S. Federal Aviation Administration (FAA)
www.faa.gov/education/educator_resources/educators_corner/index.cfm?item=kid
The U.S. FAA site for students includes activities, word puzzles, and experiments based on the history and future of air travel.

BOOKS

Bos, Samone, Phil Hunt, and Andrea Mills. *Go! The Whole World of Transportation.* Dorling Kindersley (2006)

Bowden, Rob. *Twenty-First Century Debates: Transportation.* Wayland (2004)

Graham, Ian. *Designed for Success: Superboats.* Heinemann (2008)

Graham, Ian. *Mighty Machines: Aircraft.* Franklin Watts (2009)

Herbst, Judith. *The History of Transportation.* Twenty-First Century Books (2005)

Morris, Mark. *The Cutting Edge: Transportation – High Speed, Power, and Performance.* Heinemann (2006)

Oxlade, Chris. *Illustrated Science Encyclopedia: Transportation.* Lorenz Books (2003)

Oxlade, Chris. *Mighty Machines: Trains.* Franklin Watts (2009)

Machines Rule!: On the Road. Parker, Steve. Franklin Watts (2008)

Zimmermann, Karl. *Ocean Liners.* Boyds Mills Press (2009)

Publisher's note to educators and parents:
Our editors have carefully reviewed these web sites to ensure that they are suitable for children. Many web sites change, however, and we cannot guarantee that a site's future contents will continue to meet our high standards of quality and educational value. Be advised that children should be closely supervised whenever they access the Internet.

INDEX

Page numbers in **BOLD** refer to illustrations and charts.

Advanced Driver Assistance Systems (ADAS) 42, 43
airbags 40, 43
Airbus 47, **47**
aircraft 7, 44–51, **45**, **47**, **49**, **50**, 52, 58
   cargo **50**, 50–51
   early history 44–45, **45**
   jet 46–47, **47**
   passenger 45–48, **47**, **49**, 51
   supersonic 49
air lubrication 52
antilock braking system (ABS) 41
Antonov 225 **50**, 51
aviation fuel 47

ballast tanks 13
batteries 9, 32, 36, 56–57
bicycles 32
biofuels 38–39
Blériot, Louis 44
Boeing 46, 47
bulk cargo 16–17
buses 31, **37**

canals 4, 10–12, **11**, 20
cars 7, 8, **8**, 30, 31, 32–43, **33**, **35**, **41**, 52, 58
   accidents 40–43, **41**
   electric 9, 56–57
   hybrid 36
   hydrogen 57
   safety 40–43
catalytic converters 35
climate change 8–9, 30, 35, 48, 56
coal 6, 7, 8, 9, 10, 16, 22, 24, 32
Concorde 49
congestion **8**, 31, 34, 59
crash tests **40**, 41
cruise control systems 42, 43

de Havilland 46
diesel 7, 9, 24, 34, 39

electricity 5, 9, 24, 26–30, 32, 36, 39, 56, 57
ethanol 38, 39, **39**
Exxon Valdez 17

Flying Scotsman **22**, 23
Ford Model-T 33, 40
Ford, Henry 33
fossil fuels 7–9, 38, 39, 56, 57, 59

gasoline 7, 9, 32, 34, 36, 38, 39
global warming 9
Grand Canal, China 10
Great Britain 12
greenhouse gases 9, 47

horses 4, 7, 22, 30, 33
hydrogen fuel cells 36, 57

Industrial Revolution 5, 10, 12
internal combustion engine 7, 24, 32, 36

jet engines 46

Lindbergh, Charles 44, **45**
locks 10, **11**

Mallard 23
mass production 33, **33**

oil 5, 7, 8, 9, 13, 30, 34–39, 56
   spills 16, **16**, 17
   tankers 16–17

Plimsoll, Samuel 14
pollution 8, 16, **16**, 21, 24, 31, 32, 36, 55
Prestige 16
propellers 12–13

roads 5, 7, **8**, 10, 22, 31, 32–43, 51, 52, 55
Rocket **6**, 22

seat belts 40, 43
severe acute respiratory syndrome (SARS) 48, **49**
ship canals 11
ships 4, 5, 6, 7, 10–21, 52, 58
   cargo 13, 15–17
   container 15, **15**, 16, 17
   cruise **20**, 20–21
   ferries **18**, 18–19
   hovercraft 18–19
   hydrofoils 18–19
   paddle boats 12, 13, **13**
   speedboats 20
   steam-powered 12–14, **13**
   supertankers 16–17, 52
   yachts 20
Skycar 56, **56**
solar power 36, 54, 57
space travel 50, 52, **58**, 59
speed bumps 42

speed cameras 42, **42**
steam engines 5, 6, **6**, 7, **22**, 22–24
steam power 5, 6, 22
   ships 12–14, **13**
   trains **6**, **22**, 22–24
Stephenson, George 22
submarines 13, **53**
   supersonic 52–53, **53**
subway systems 9, **29**, 29–30, 31

TGV **27**, 27–28
Titanic 14, **14**
trains 6, **6**, 7, 9, **22**, 22–31, **25**, **27**, **28**, **29**, **54**, 58
   aero-train 54, **54**
   diesel 24
   diesel-electric 24
   electric 26–28
   funicular 25
   high-speed 26–28, **27**
   light rail 30–31
   maglev 28, **28**
   monorails 31
   rack-and-pinion 25, **25**
   steam **6**, **22**, 22–24
   underground **29**, 29–30, 31
   vacuum tube 54–55
trams 9, 30–31, **31**
trucks 34, **35**

Watt, James 5, 6, 7
wheels 4, **4**, 25, 41
wind power 54, 57
Wright, Orville and Wilbur 44

About the Author
Joseph Harris earned a degree at St. Anne's College in Oxford, United Kingdom. He did post-graduate research before becoming a freelance writer. He writes books for young people about history.

About the Consultant
Miles Hudson is a high school science teacher and author of many science and physics textbooks for young adults.